THE GRAPEFRUIT
A NEW YC

Unlocking The Weight Loss Potential Of Grapefruit: The Ultimate Diet Companion [Grapefruit]

KELVIN EDWARD

Contents

CHAPTER ONE

An Introductory

The Grapefruit Diet, often called the Hollywood Diet, is consuming either a grapefruit or a glass of grapefruit juice before each meal in order to shed excess pounds.

Its initial popularity peaked in the 1930s, and the diet has since had occasional resurgences.

The average duration of the Grapefruit Diet (a low-calorie eating plan) is 10-12 days.

Protein-rich foods like eggs, meat, and fish, as well as non-starchy vegetables, tend to be the mainstays

4

of this type of diet, along with a restricted daily caloric intake. Because of its purported fat-burning enzymes, the diet also calls for a serving of grapefruit or grapefruit juice with each meal.

The Grapefruit Diet, so the argument goes, can help you shed up to 10 pounds in just 14 days.

The diet's rigorous calorie restriction can lead to vitamin deficits and other health concerns, and there is no evidence to support the concept that grapefruit has any special fat-burning capabilities.

As a result, any weight reduction obtained by the Grapefruit program is likely to be restored once the program is discontinued.

Before beginning any weight loss program, it is recommended that you talk to a doctor.

Grapefruit Diet: Theory And Practice

The Grapefruit Diet is a low-calorie eating plan that emphasizes including grapefruit or grapefruit juice with each meal in order to aid in weight loss.

For 10–12 days, you eat a restricted diet that emphasizes protein-rich foods like eggs, meat, and fish, as well as non-starchy vegetables.

Because of its purported fat-burning enzymes, the diet also calls for a serving of grapefruit or grapefruit juice with each meal.

There is no scientific evidence to suggest that grapefruit has any unique fat-burning characteristics, and the exact process through which it can help weight loss is not well understood.

Grapefruit, on the other hand, has few calories but is packed with healthy minerals like vitamin C and fiber, which may make you feel full on less food.

Most people need more than 1,000 calories per day to maintain their weight, however the Grapefruit Diet often delivers less than 1,000 calories per day.

Fast weight reduction may result from such severe calorie restriction, but the health risks may not outweigh the benefits.

Because of the significant calorie restriction required, any weight loss experienced while following the Grapefruit Diet is likely to be just temporary.

Making positive changes to your diet, exercise routine, and relationship with food can lead to long-term weight loss success.

CHAPTER TWO

The Grapefruit Diet: Pros And Cons

There are possible benefits and hazards to the Grapefruit Diet, making it a contentious weight loss approach.

Benefits:

• The Grapefruit Diet, because it is low in calories, can lead to quick weight loss in the short term. It has been reported that some people lose as much as 10 pounds in just two weeks.

• Protein-rich foods and non-starchy veggies are frequently featured on the Grapefruit Diet since they are low in fat and contribute to weight loss.

• Low in calories and high in beneficial elements like vitamin C and fiber, grapefruit is a smart addition to any healthy diet.

Risks:

• Because of its low calorie content, the Grapefruit Diet may not supply enough of some nutrients, including vitamins and minerals.

• Dehydration: The combination of the diet's diuretic effect and the reduction in fluid intake can have this effect.

• The high calorie restriction and lack of vital nutrients on the Grapefruit Diet can lead to weariness and weakness.

• Because of the extreme nature of the food restrictions imposed by the Grapefruit Diet, many essential nutrients may be missed.

• Any weight loss obtained while on the Grapefruit Diet is likely to be recovered after the diet is ended because it is not a sustainable approach to lose weight in the long term.

Overall, the dangers and potential negative health implications make the Grapefruit Diet unsuitable as a long-term weight management approach. Before beginning any weight loss program, it is recommended that you talk to a doctor.

Grapefruit Diet Approved Snacks

As part of its low-calorie plan, the Grapefruit Diet recommends eating a grapefruit or drinking grapefruit juice with every meal.

The Grapefruit Diet typically consists of the following foods:

Protein:

• Eggs.

• Meats (poultry, beef, turkey, etc.).

• Foods such as salmon, tuna, and other fish.

• Cheese.

• Seeds and nuts.

Vegetables without starch:

• Spinach, kale, lettuce, and other leafy greens.

• Vegetables such as broccoli, cauliflower, cabbage, tomatoes, bell peppers, carrots, cucumbers, and a variety of others may be found at almost any supermarket.

• You can eat or drink a grapefruit or grapefruit juice.

Beverages:

• Coffee or tea without sugar.

It is worth noting that the Grapefruit Diet is a highly restrictive eating plan that cuts out a wide variety of nutritious foods.

It is crucial to make sure you are getting enough of the right kinds of vitamins, minerals, and fiber while on this eating plan. Long-term adherence to this diet is also discouraged because of the risk of vitamin deficits and related health issues.

Before beginning any weight loss program, it is recommended that you talk to a doctor.

The Grapefruit Diet: Foods To Avoid

The Grapefruit Diet is an extremely limited eating plan that excludes a wide variety of foods, notably those high in carbohydrates and fat.

Some common dietary items to avoid while on the Grapefruit Diet include:

Carbohydrates:

• Cereals, grains, legumes (beans, lentils, etc.), and starchy foods like bread, pasta, rice, potatoes, and cereal.

Fats:

• Oils (olive oil, vegetable oil, etc.).

• Butter.

• Margarine.

• Avocado.

• Nuts and seeds (with the exception of a select few allowed on the diet).

Sweeteners:

• Ingredients: Sugar, Honey, Syrup, and Artificial Sweeteners.

Beverages:

• Drinks: soda, juice (other than grapefruit), and water.

• Alcohol.

It is worth noting that the Grapefruit Diet is a highly restrictive eating plan that cuts out a wide variety of nutritious foods.

It is crucial to make sure you are getting enough of the right kinds of vitamins, minerals, and fiber while on this eating plan. Long-term adherence to this diet is also discouraged because of the risk of vitamin deficits and related health issues.

Before beginning any weight loss program, it is recommended that you talk to a doctor.

CHAPTER THREE

Planned Grapefruit-Based Meal Example

Here's what a typical day's worth of the Grapefruit Diet may look like:

Breakfast:

• Black coffee or tea (no sugar or cream) with two hard-boiled eggs

• Chicken breasts on the grill.

• A green salad dressed with lemon juice and olive oil, topped with tomatoes and cucumbers.

• One-Half Grapefruit.

As a snack, try:

• Some almonds.

Grilled salmon, steamed broccoli, and half a grapefruit for dinner, followed by:

• Unsweetened grapefruit juice in a tall glass.

It is worth noting that the Grapefruit Diet is a highly restrictive eating plan that cuts out a wide variety of nutritious foods.

It is crucial to make sure you are getting enough of the right kinds of vitamins, minerals, and fiber while on this eating plan.

Long-term adherence to this diet is also discouraged because of the risk of vitamin deficits and related health issues. Before beginning any weight loss program, it is recommended that you talk to a doctor.

Dietary Grapefruit Recommendations

Here are some suggestions for making the most of the Grapefruit Diet:

• Prepare your meals in advance: If you plan your meals in advance, you will be more likely to eat healthily and not stray from your diet.

• Drink lots of water throughout the day because the Grapefruit Diet might cause dehydration due to its diuretic impact.

• Make physical activity a regular part of your routine; it will boost your metabolism and help you lose weight more effectively.

• Keep track of how many calories you consume. Since the Grapefruit Diet is so low in calories, it is essential to keep an eye on your calorie intake to prevent nutrient deficiencies and other health issues.

• Pay attention to how you feel. Signs of being undernourished include a lack of strength, weariness, and dizziness. If you notice a change in how you feel, it is time to reevaluate your diet.

• The Grapefruit Diet is a fairly limited eating plan, so keep in mind that you may not be able to maintain it indefinitely.

It is not healthy to expect drastic weight loss from eating less and exercising more.

• Seek the advice of a medical expert: Before beginning any weight loss program, including the Grapefruit Diet, it is recommended that you speak with a medical expert.

They can check your health before and after you start the diet to see if it is a good fit.

Conclusion

The Grapefruit Diet is a calorie-controlled eating plan that requires you to consume either a whole grapefruit or a glass of grapefruit juice with every meal.

This diet may help some individuals lose weight, but it is also quite restrictive and might not give you what you need to stay healthy in the long run.

Make sure you are eating a healthy, well-rounded diet and getting plenty of exercise before starting any weight loss program.

THE END

Printed in Great Britain
by Amazon